BLACK DIAMONDS BY SEA

North-East Sailing Colliers 1780-1880

The wind at North, a pleasant gale,
Below the Middens we make sail;
'Steamboat ahoy! Let-go the warp;
Come haul it in my lads, look sharp!'

Dick Keys and Ken Smith

Newcastle Libraries & Information Service, in association with Tyne & Wear Museums

Acknowledgements

The authors would like to thank Tyne & Wear Museums for their advice and support, and the staff of the Local Studies Section, Newcastle Libraries & Information Service, for their unfailing assistance and courtesy.

Illustrations acknowledgements:
Gateshead Libraries & Arts: page 17;
The Illustrated London News Picture Library: pages 27, 37, 41, 44;
Dick Keys: pages 5, 10, 16, 19, 34, 45, 48;
Newcastle Libraries & Information Service: pages 4, 8, 20, 21, 23, 38, 40, 42, and the miscellaneous engravings;
South Shields Metropolitan Borough Council: pages 6, 7, 39;
Tyne & Wear Museums: front and back cover illustrations, and those on pages 12, 15, 22, 30, 46.

British Library Cataloguing in Publication data: a catalogue record for this book is available from the British Library.

Printed by Bailes the Printer, Houghton le Spring

Front cover:
Shipping at the Mouth of the Tyne, 1845, by John Scott

Back cover:
Lifeboat off the South Pier, South Shields, 1861, by John Scott

Other books by Dick Keys and Ken Smith published by Newcastle Libraries & Information Service:

Down Elswick Slipways: Armstrong's Ships and People 1884-1918, Newcastle City Libraries, 1996.

From Walker to the World: Charles Mitchell's Low Walker Shipyard, Newcastle Libraries & Information Service, 1997.

By Ian Rae and Ken Smith:

Swans of the Tyne, Newcastle City Libraries with North Tyneside Libraries, 1994.

Built with Pride: Tyne Ships 1969-1994, Newcastle City Libraries, 1995.

By Ken Smith:

Mauretania: Pride of the Tyne, Newcastle Libraries & Information Service, with Tyne & Wear Museums, 1997.

Turbinia: the Story of Charles Parsons and his Ocean Greyhound, Newcastle Libraries & Information Service with Tyne & Wear Museums, 1996.

A free catalogue and further information is available from

Publications
City Library
Princess Square
Newcastle upon Tyne
NE99 1DX

Contents

Illustrations

A brig, left, and a brigantine lie together off the Gateshead shore of the Tyne. Probably late 19th century.

~Coal Cargoes~

For hundreds of years the coal trade of the rivers Tyne and Wear in North-East England was dominated by the sailing colliers – the little wooden ships which carried their cargoes of 'black diamonds' southwards to London and to other ports of Britain and beyond.

The economy of the North-East was based upon the rich coal seams of Northumberland and County Durham, mined by the area's hard-working and spirited people. From Medieval times onwards coal was exported from the region to feed a steadily expanding market and most of it was carried away by sea in the colliers.

In the year ending Michaelmas 1592 a total of 91,420 tons of coal was recorded as being exported on the coastal routes from the Tyne. One hundred years later the amount had quadrupled. By 1800 it had reached nearly 1.5 million tons. Twenty years later the two million mark was passed. The number of departures from the river by loaded colliers on coastal voyages ran into thousands each year. In 1830, for example, there were 11,226 such sailings.

By the late 18th century colliers were typically the two-masted, square-sailed brigs and their closely-related variant, the 'snow', which featured a third, short mast immediately behind the main mast, but carried the same sails. Customs officials might refer to 'brigs and snows' but the seamen who manned them called them all simply 'brigs'. Another variant of the brig was the brigantine, which carried square sails on the fore mast only. These ships were generally broad in the beam with bluff bows and had a good cargo carrying capacity for their relatively short length.

Between 1830 and the end of the sailing ship era approximately 1,450 snows, 875 brigs, 145 brigantines and 455 schooners were owned on Tyneside.

The crews spoke of 'Shields Harbour', including both North and South Shields in this description since ships were moored

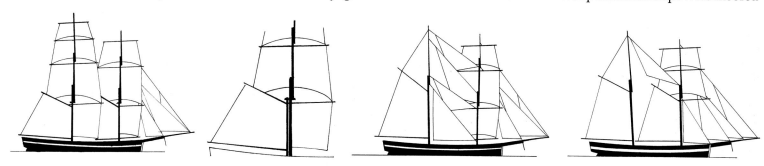

North-East collier sailing rigs. Far left, a brig, carrying two masts with square sails on each mast. Second left, the main mast of a snow, which features a spar immediately behind the main mast to which the try sail (or spanker) is attached. Otherwise identical to a brig. Third left, a brigantine, carrying square sails on the fore mast only. The main mast is fore-and-aft rigged. Far right, a schooner, with fore-and-aft sails on both masts and carrying a square top-sail and top-gallant sail on the fore mast.

*An unidentified snow under tow. This ship might possibly be the **Azalea**, built in 1858 on the Tyne. In 1867 she was sold to Blyth owners. Two years later she was wrecked in the Baltic. The ship might also be the **Azela**, built in Newcastle in 1858 and owned by J. Eltringham of Blyth in the 1880s.*

*The brig **Annie***. *A 281-ton vessel of that name was built in 1858 at Sunderland for William Pippet, of South Shields. She was 102ft long. On November 12 1883 the **Annie** sailed from the Tyne with coal for Aberdeen but was later reported missing.*

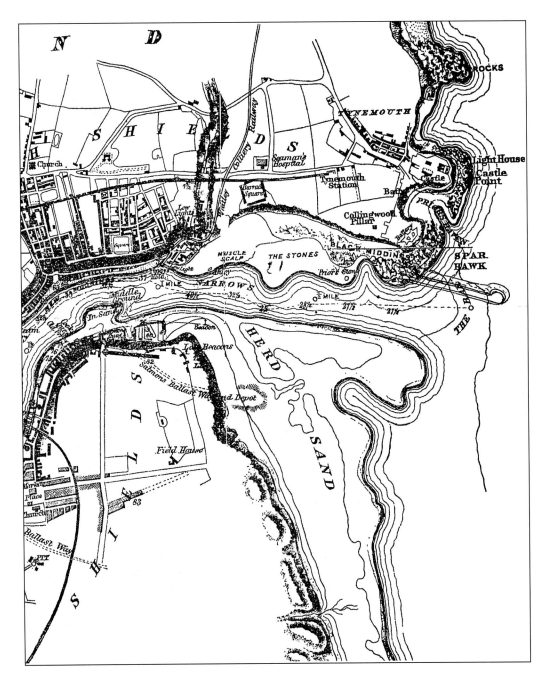

A mid-19th century map of the mouth of the Tyne, unprotected by the two large piers built in later years. However, an early pier is shown projecting from the northern end of the river mouth. The extensive Herd Sand can be seen to the south. It proved to be the graveyard of many sailing ships and men, driven ashore by gales or storms. To the north, below the Collingwood Monument, are the notorious Black Middens Rocks and the Spanish Battery and Castle Point headlands, further perils for colliers dependent on the vagaries of the wind.

on both sides of the river mouth. To a sailor entering the Tyne it was all one harbour.

These mariners who sailed in and out of Shields were a hardy breed of men who braved the constant danger of shipwreck. Each year men lost their lives when storms or gales drove vessels onto the rocks, sands or shingle of the East Coast.

The mouth of the Tyne contained two particularly treacherous dangers for colliers, the Herd Sand at South Shields and the Black Middens rocks at Tynemouth. Many ships also went ashore on the rocks of the Spanish Battery. In addition, the Tyne Bar, a ridge of sand and shingle running beneath the surface at the entrance to the river, was a notorious obstacle to shipping at low tide. The approach to the harbour was therefore fraught with hazards in the shape of reefs and shallows.

A further peril which haunted seamen in the North-East coal trade during the late 1700s and early 1800s was the press gang. Such men were highly sought after by the Royal Navy because of their sailing skills and experience. A spell in the Tyne or Wear's collier fleet was considered an excellent training ground for service in His Majesty's warships. During the wars with France press gangs operated in major North-East ports. North Shields, South Shields, Sunderland and Newcastle were among the towns targeted by these official gangs of the Navy's Impress Service. Not surprisingly, the seamen grew to regard them with a mixture of fear and detestation.

On top of this, there were French privateers to contend with. These were privately-owned ships which would attack enemy merchant vessels and capture them as prizes. Their aim was to contribute towards their country's war effort by wrecking the trade and depleting the wealth of their foe. They carried out their raids with the approval of their own government. Understandably, the collier seamen viewed these opportunist crews as little better than pirates exploiting the wars for their own ends. Yet it should be remembered that Britain had her own privateers.

A Tyne collier's voyage would begin on the river after coal had been loaded on to her from a keel boat or had cascaded into her hold from a spout protruding from the end of a staith (jetty). Alternatively, it might be dropped into the hold from a waggon lowered to deck level from a staith.

But before the development of steam railways, most colliers were loaded from the keels which brought their cargoes to ships anchored at Shields and in the lower reaches of the river.

It was impossible to navigate a sailing ship above Newcastle's low 18th century stone bridge and its predecessor, the medieval bridge. Keels therefore retained the advantage for many years of being able to bring coal from stretches of the river above the bridge. However, the coming of the steam railways meant that 'black diamonds' could be carried to staiths in the lower reaches which had been built to take ships. This development led to the gradual disappearance of keels from the river.

The round trip from the Tyne to London and back, which included the passage time each way, time spent discharging and taking aboard ballast, usually occupied about one month, but was sometimes much longer. Colliers could be held up in the Thames for many weeks if winds were unfavourable. In March 1864, for instance, it was reported that some colliers were taking seven or eight weeks to complete their round voyages to London and back.

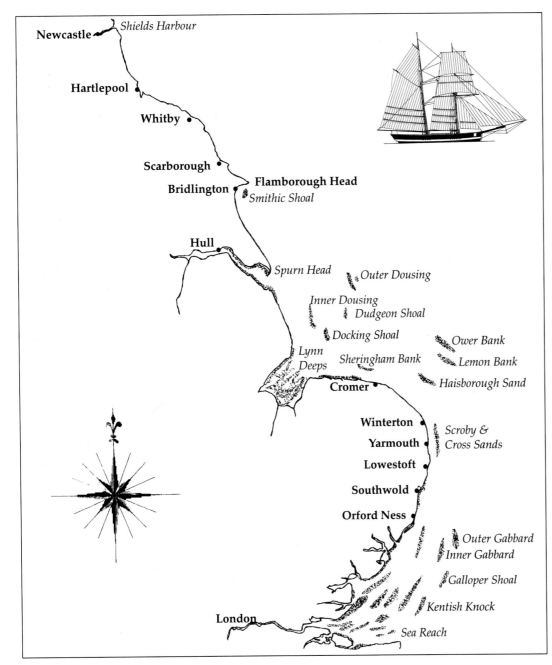

Newcastle — Shields Harbour

Hartlepool

Whitby

Scarborough

Bridlington — Flamborough Head
Smithic Shoal

Hull

Spurn Head — Outer Dousing

Inner Dousing
Dudgeon Shoal

Docking Shoal — Ower Bank

Lynn Deeps — Sheringham Bank — Lemon Bank

Haisborough Sand

Cromer

Winterton — Scroby & Cross Sands

Yarmouth

Lowestoft

Southwold

Orford Ness

Outer Gabbard
Inner Gabbard

Galloper Shoal

London — Kentish Knock

Sea Reach

The East Coast of England from Shields Harbour to the Thames.

The sailing colliers met many hazards on the journey to London and other ports. The sands off Lincolnshire, Norfolk, and in the approach to the Thames were particularly treacherous. They ended the careers of numerous ships from the Tyne, Wear and Tees. Any gale or wind blowing from the north-east, east or south-east could put a collier at risk of being blown onto the sands. The sands could also be friendly. The Cross and Scroby Sands off Yarmouth provided shelter to ships anchored in Yarmouth Roads. The large volume of collier traffic along the East Coast greatly increased the chances of shipwrecks.

Extracts from the log of the schooner *Sally*, which regularly made the trip from Shields to London, may be found on page 35.

Likewise, sailing from the Tyne could be greatly delayed by calms or adverse winds. Shields harbour would be crowded with shipping for days or even weeks as the vessels awaited favourable weather. Indeed, the advent of a good wind to take them south would result in a vast array of colliers all departing together in what must have been an impressive sight.

For example, in April 1808 it was reported that in the space of two days more than 100 loaded colliers left Shields for different ports in the South. Most of these vessels had been detained at the mouth of the Tyne for nearly three weeks by easterly winds. Conversely, a strong westerly wind could prevent a collier from entering Shields.

Once on her way to her destination port, gales might blow a ship completely off course. To be driven aground on to a lee shore of the East Coast was one of the most common accidents. But it was naturally possible to be swept away in more than one direction. In February 1854 the South Shields owners of the brig *Royal Union* received a letter from her captain telling them that their vessel had arrived in Gothenburg, Sweden. The ship had gone missing while on a coal voyage from the Tyne to London and back.

The *Royal Union* had left the Tyne in early December 1853. All went well until the homeward voyage when she ran into a severe east-south-east gale which drove before it a large fleet of light and laden ships. Some ended up as far north as Aberdeen. After being blown past the Tyne entrance in early January, the *Royal Union* eventually dropped anchor in a precarious position off North Berwick, at the southern entrance to the Firth of Forth.

Just as the weather was thought to be moderating, and there was a chance of being able to beat back to the Tyne, another gale came roaring in from the north-west. Slipping her last anchor (three had already been lost), the *Royal Union* was driven out into the North Sea. Nothing was heard of her until the arrival of her master's letter the following month in which he told of the 'seamanship and patient endurance' of his men while 'knocking about' in the North Sea for many weeks. The hardships endured by the crew must have been considerable.

Another example of a collier blown completely off course was the *Jenny*, which sailed from Shields with a cargo of coal bound for Harwich in early 1801. She was driven by adverse winds across the North Sea to the coast of Norway. The *Jenny* sailed into the Norwegian port of Arendal and managed to sell her coal. She then took on a cargo of timber and eventually reached Whitby.

Many, but by no means all, ships in the collier trade were Tyne or Wear-owned. One of numerous examples of such vessels was the Tyne-owned snow *Corinthian*, built in 1824 by John Laing & Son at South Shields. It is recorded that on June 14 1831 she arrived off Gravesend in the Thames with 344 tons of coal on board. She was just one of 223 colliers to enter the Thames within the previous fortnight, most from the North-East coast.

There was a 16-day delay before her cargo was sold, after which her master would probably have received orders for her to proceed to a buoy further up river where the coal would have been 'jumped out' by gangs of coal-whippers and transferred to barges for delivery to various wharfs and creeks on the Thames. Coal-whipping was a method of unloading whereby the cargo was rapidly lifted from the hold in baskets using the combined weight of four men who jumped from a raised platform, each clasping an individual rope leading to a single line or runner, to which a basket of coal was attached. By July 6 all the *Corinthian*'s cargo had been discharged – 22 days after arrival.

The *Corinthian* would almost certainly have returned to the Tyne loaded with ballast to provide her with stability. The materials used as ballast varied, but colliers coming from the Thames generally took aboard shingle, stones or chalk.

Ships returning home were sometimes referred to as 'light' colliers, indicating that they were carrying ballast, around 60 or 70 tons of it, as opposed to a coal cargo of perhaps 200 or 300 tons. Once she reached the Tyne a ship would unload her ballast on the banks of the river. Sometimes this material fell into the water or was dumped unofficially into the river, thus contributing to silting problems.

The record for the fastest round voyage from the Tyne to London and back by a sailing collier must surely go to the brig *Hilda*. Under the command of John Firbank, of South Shields, who was also the ship's owner, she left the Tyne on December 7 1862 and arrived back in the river seven days later. It was an exceptional performance. She had discharged 399 tons of coal in the Regent's Canal and taken in 70 tons of ballast for the homeward trip.

A collier brig lies off Felling, Gateshead, in this peaceful scene. Artist: J.W. Carmichael. Engraver: Lambert & Collard.

For consistent and trouble-free voyages by sail, the record of the 245-ton brig *Phesdo*, of North Shields, is unlikely to have been beaten. Between 1831 and 1842 she made 100 London voyages, all under the command of Robert Elliot, without sustaining any damage in excess of £20.

The year's work performed in 1849 by the 49-year-old snow *Walker*, belonging to George Hall, a North Shields grocer, was regarded as very good. She had made nine runs to London, one to Hamburg and another across the Atlantic to New Brunswick in Canada. It is possible that on this Canadian voyage she took coal outward bound and carried a cargo of timber homeward.

Owners often withdrew their vessels from the London coal run when they could be more profitably employed elsewhere. It should also be noted that a great deal of coal was exported from the Tyne to destinations overseas, especially the Baltic, Mediterranean and near Continental ports.

The crew of the veteran *Walker* had proved that in their small ship they could cross a great ocean as well as navigate the familiar waters of the East Coast. The Tyne's collier sailors were clearly men of immense courage and skill.

~Striking Seamen~

The late 18th and early 19th centuries witnessed a series of strikes by Tyne seamen demanding higher wages. In December 1800 it was reported that several colliers were leaving Shields harbour when they were approached by boats from the shore manned by strikers. The men were demanding wages of 11 guineas per voyage and their aim was to prevent any ships from leaving the port until their claim had been settled.

However, the *Good Design*, an armed ship under the command of a Captain Brown, intervened. The captain ordered his boats to be manned and armed with the intention of foiling the striking seamen. The tactic worked. On seeing the warship's boats lowered, the strikers made for the shore and dispersed. The colliers were then able to sail out to sea without further problem.

Two years later the Tyne was again hit by strikes. On June 6 1802 the *Newcastle Courant* reported: 'Since Saturday night the sailors on the Tyne have been disorderly, on account of wages, taking most of the men out of all the ships in which their demands were not acceded to, and ill treat those who declined to join them.' After a few days, the ship owners agreed to a wage rate of four guineas for the London voyage and three pounds per month for voyages to the Baltic.

It would appear that the authorities were worried by this discontent. On June 19 1802 it was reported that His Majesty's brig cutter *Cruiser* had arrived at Shields 'to assist in keeping the peace of the port'.

November 1802 saw more unrest. Striking seamen dragged crews out of the ships in Shields harbour to prevent them from sailing. In talks with the Mayor of Newcastle and employers, which were held at North Shields, representatives of the men complained of low wages and a compromise settlement was suggested. It appeared that peace had been restored and if the ships had been able to sail away without delay further trouble might have been averted.

But it was not to be. Unfavourable winds kept the loaded vessels from proceeding to sea. The sailors again protested about the low level of wages and resumed picketing ships in the harbour to prevent them from sailing. Those men who refused to join the strikers were marched through the streets with their faces blackened and their jackets turned inside out.

At about this time, similar unrest was reported at Sunderland, where those who would not join the strike were also subjected to 'face blackening'. At this port the wages were eventually settled at the rate of five guineas per voyage.

Trouble flared again in the autumn of 1806. Seamen returning from whaling expeditions in Greenland waters had arrived in the Tyne. They spent their wages enjoying themselves but afterwards sought work on the colliers. However, the Greenland men were clearly unhappy with the level of wages being offered and soon they were stopping ships from putting to sea in an effort to win higher rates. It was reported that if vessels sailed, they were boarded by the Greenland men who dropped their anchors and persuaded or forced their crews to join them.

Not surprisingly, the authorities took a dim view of such proceedings. They regarded strikes as riots. When it was reported that 'seditious and inflammatory' papers had been

stuck up at Shields, the Mayor of Newcastle intervened and soldiers were called in to 'restore order'. Two troops of the Royal Scots Greys were drafted into North Shields and two rifle companies of the Sussex Militia were sent from Whitburn Barracks to South Shields. The *Newcastle Courant* told readers: 'By accounts from Shields yesterday morning, all was quiet amongst those people, but it is only the hand of power which keeps them so.'

In the same article the *Courant* declared: 'The late Lord Hugh Seymour used to say that insubordination and contempt of the law amongst the seamen in the coal trade was one of the springs of the rebellion in His Majesty's Navy at the Nore near ten years since, therefore suppression in the bud is necessary, and in no part of the United Kingdom is a strict police so much wanted as on the Tyne.'

In February 1813 it was reported that nearly 30 'riotous' seamen were taken by a press gang at Shields and lodged in HMS *Transit*, bound for the naval anchorage at the Nore. This was probably not the only time that press gangs were used as a method of suppressing strikes, unrest or disorder.

Another dispute broke out in September 1815. This time it was at Sunderland and once again the seamen were stopping vessels from putting to sea. Unemployment is likely to have been a factor in this strike, for the crews were demanding that the ships should take on an extra hand, or two, according to

tonnage. They were also seeking higher wages. Within just over two weeks the dispute was reported to have been settled amicably, but by this time discontent had spread to the Tyne.

The demand on the Tyne was for the ships to take on five men and one boy for every 100 tons. Again, better wages were also sought. Those seamen willing to sail were taken off their ships by the strikers. Some men appear to have used the situation as an opportunity to settle old scores – a midshipman formerly belonging to a press gang was tarred and feathered.

At the end of September it was reported that the strike had resumed on the Wear and was still in progress on the Tyne. The striking sailors had by this time formed a committee and those who broke the rules of the stoppage were paraded through the streets in the usual way with faces blackened and jackets turned inside out. Shipping at Shields was largely halted by the dispute. Those few vessels which did manage to depart had received permission from the strike committee. They were required to hoist a special flag to indicate that they had been allowed to sail.

The authorities were not amused. They called in the Royal Navy in an attempt to suppress the strike and restore normal trading. HMS *Griper* and HMS *Tartarus* arrived in the Tyne in October 1815 and their officers and men assisted some ships in getting to sea. Representatives of the seamen met the Mayor of Newcastle at the Guildhall but the dispute remained unresolved.

Shields harbour was by this time badly overcrowded with vessels and a number, including *Griper* and *Tartarus,* broke from their moorings. About 20 ships were damaged as a result, including many colliers.

Soon the *Griper* and *Tartarus* were joined by other warships. In addition, Royal Marines were brought by sea from Portsmouth to Shields and soldiers of the Westminster Militia sailed into Sunderland. By early November there were signs that the strike was over. The seamen may well have been cowed by the intervention of the Navy and the military.

Artist J.W. Carmichael's depiction of the river mouth at North Shields. Engraver: Lambert & Collard.

On the 4th of the month it was reported that 150 colliers were due to clear Shields harbour within the following week and that 40 colliers from the North-East had already arrived at Portsmouth.

Despite what appears to have been the collapse of the strike, warships were stationed in the Tyne as a precaution against disturbances for at least a year afterwards.

However, although violence and intimidation were a regrettable feature of the seamen's disputes, it is not surprising that feelings ran so high. Unemployment following the end of the Napoleonic Wars had caused hardship and appears to have driven down wages. Seafaring in the coal trade was hard and dangerous work. It was small wonder that the men sought adequate recompense when they daily risked their lives in a battle against the elements. Frequently men sailed from the Tyne and the Wear but never returned alive after losing that battle.

*Left, two collier brigantines on the Wear, the **Alice Richardson** and **Eliza Emma**. Right, a topsail schooner under tow by the tug **Surprise**.*

A topsail schooner lies off the Gateshead shore of the Tyne. All Saints Church and Newcastle can be seen to the right with Robert Stephenson's High Level Bridge in the background. The photograph probably dates from the late 19th century.

~Ships in Peril~

In 1789 the collier *Adventure* was driven on to the Herd Sand at South Shields by a strong gale. The ship was only a few hundred yards from the beach but the sea was so rough South Shields boatmen were unable to attempt a rescue. Most of the *Adventure*'s crew were lost. A crowd of local people gathered on the shore, helpless to intervene because of that fateful few hundred yards of raging sea. Some of the unfortunate crewmen clung to the rigging but then fell into the waves.

The tragedy which befell this ship and other vessels at the mouth of the Tyne led to the development at South Shields of the first purpose-built lifeboat, *The Original*. This oar-pulled vessel saved several hundred lives during a long career between 1790 and 1830. Other early lifeboats based at the mouth of the river, such as the *Northumberland* and the *Tyne*, also did sterling work in what was clearly a much-needed service for seamen in peril. Shipwreck was an all too common occurrence along the East Coast, with colliers, not surprisingly, featuring prominently in the toll of accidents.

In early April 1799 a fierce storm raged in the North Sea and the colliers on passage along the East Coast suffered many casualties, both in terms of ships and men. Within the three days before the storm over 200 vessels had departed from Shields and Sunderland, most of which had to face the full power of wind and sea. Soon reports were coming in of ships being driven ashore, often with fatal consequences.

Among the ships wrecked in this way were the *Elizabeth*, of North Shields, which was lost near Whitburn with all hands; the *Auspicious*, and another vessel from Sunderland which were wrecked off Newbiggin with several of their crew members reported drowned; and the *Ranger*, of Scarborough, lost with all hands on only her fifth voyage.

Besides the *Auspicious*, no less than 12 other ships were said to have been wrecked between Blyth and Holy Island. They were the *John*, of South Shields, one crewman saved; the *George and Mary*, of Sunderland, lost on Cresswell Sands with all hands except the captain; the *Active*, of Sunderland, all hands lost; the *Friends*, of Blakeney, Norfolk, crew drowned; the *Blessing* of Kings Lynn, Norfolk, a boy reported drowned; the *Mayflower*, of Kings Lynn, crew saved; the *Joseph and Mary*, of Newcastle, several crewmen drowned; the *Thetis*, of North Shields, crew lost; the *Charming Harriet*, of South Shields, five saved, six drowned; the *Elizabeth and Margaret*, of North Shields, crew drowned; the *Gemini*, of Blyth, crew saved; and the *Jamaica*, of London, crew saved.

To the south of Sunderland the storm had claimed more casualties: the *Experiment*, of Stockton, a new ship, was lost near Seaham and all hands perished; the *Maria* was reported on shore near Seaham; the *Francis*, was wrecked off the Tees, but the crew saved; a sloop, whose name was not reported, also came to grief near Seaham with the loss of all the crew; and lastly a Sunderland ship was wrecked, whose name is also unclear, from which at least several men were saved.

Within a week the bodies of the many seamen who had perished in the storm began to be washed up on the North-East coast. They were buried by the different parishes in which they were found.

Late January 1802 witnessed another tempest of great

*The barque **Diamante** lies wrecked on 26th March 1898 on the Black Middens Rocks. She was entering the Tyne with pit props from Sandefjord. Eight of the crew were rescued with rocket apparatus. Far left, a breach can be seen in the North Pier as a result of the fierce storm. Pit props were a regular import cargo to the Tyne.*

The crew of the Tynemouth lifeboat man their oar-pulled vessel as men on the left point to a wreck which has hit the Black Middens rocks in the river mouth. This photograph was taken c.1870.

In December 1802, the *Advice*, of South Shields, came to grief. She was lost on the 17th of the month on Haisborough Sand, off the Norfolk coast. Her master and several crewmen were drowned. Two, however, lived to tell the tale. These men clung to a piece of wreckage and were driven out into the North Sea. They managed to survive for 18 hours until they were spotted by a Post Office packet boat which took them to Heligoland off the north German coast. They reported that a third man had also been clinging to the wreckage but through fatigue and cold he was lost before the rescue ship arrived. The survivors eventually returned to South Shields.

In early January the following year another great storm hit the waters of the East Coast which lasted for nearly two days. Beginning in the middle of the night, the winds rose until they were said to be 'a perfect hurricane', blowing from the east-south-east. This tempest was accompanied by rain and sleet. With the coming of dawn, observers on the coasts of Northumberland and County Durham noted that the sea was a mass of white and broken water.

Already, ships had begun to be swept ashore. The *Ruby*, of Newcastle, in ballast from London, was driven aground near the Bondi Carr Rocks close to Amble at 3am. The crew survived. Also lucky were the men of the new sloop *Flora*, of

power. As the wind rose three ships coming into Shields harbour were driven on to the Herd Sand, but the tide was flowing very high and they cut their anchor cables and managed to get out to sea again. However, the *Thomas and Alice*, a brig from Blyth, was also blown on to the sand. The *Northumberland* lifeboat was launched and her courageous oarsmen pulled through the huge breakers, reached the vessel and saved the entire crew. The brig remained, to be pounded by the fierce seas. Several days later, she was got off the sand by throwing part of her coals overboard, although she had suffered damage.

The harbour at Shields in a gale. A rescued ship's crew are being brought towards the shore at North Shields in a lifeboat. Wreckage from the ship floats in the rough sea, right. Below the High and Low Lights a crowd awaits the boat.

An artist's dramatic depiction of a wreck at the mouth of the Tyne. Centre, a crowd watch the stricken ship from the headland. The ruins of Tynemouth Priory stand out, along with the lighthouse tower, right, as if illuminated by lightning.

Whitby, which struck ground a little to the south of the *Ruby*. Her jib sail had been lost.

The *Sarah*, a ship from North Shields, hit rocks near Seaton House, to the north of Alnmouth. The vessel's bottom was damaged but the crew managed to reach the safety of dry land.

The *Ann*, of Sunderland, grounded on the sands near Alnmouth harbour. Again, the crew survived and it was hoped that the ship would be got off with only slight damage.

The colliers *Arno*, of South Shields, and the *Elizabeth and Mary*, of Newcastle, struck the shore near Dunstanburgh

Castle, to the north of Craster. Tragically, a boy from the *Arno* was drowned.

A ship named the *John and Robert* was reported to have weathered the storm for a whole day, but the exhausted crew found their vessel being driven mercilessly towards the coast. They tried in vain to reach the shelter of Coquet Roads. Then the ship lost her try-sail and the crew were forced to attempt anchoring near the North Steel rocks off Coquet Island.

Their problems grew when the *John and Robert* struck a submerged rock. The captain ordered the cable to be cut so that the vessel might free herself. This move proved effective and she rode clear of the rock. As the ship drifted into deep water, they dropped anchor. The crew then became aware that the vessel was seriously damaged and that she was rapidly filling with water. The decision was made to cut the cable and run the ship ashore. The *John and Robert* grounded near the mouth of the Coquet close to the Pan Rock and was seriously damaged. The crew of 14 managed after considerable effort to reach safety in the ship's boat.

At Berwick, residents awoke in the morning to find a ship at anchor off their shore being buffeted by the huge waves. She had only one mast left standing and was flying a distress flag. The seas were so high that no boat could reach them. Eventually the vessel got under way and attempted to enter the Tweed. However, she struck rocks near the river mouth. But luck was on her side and she managed to free herself and ride over them into smoother water. Spectators on the shore cheered when they saw the crew were safe.

An artist's view of the Spanish Battery headland at Tynemouth in 1886. On the left, a brigantine is being towed into the river by a paddle tug.

The vessel was the *Pearl*, of North Shields, under the command of a Captain Rose, who had a crew of 15. After this event, a fund to provide a lifeboat for Berwick was started by residents.

Meanwhile, the casualties of the storm were still mounting. A vessel named the *Hope*, which had sought the relative safety of Priors Haven, Tynemouth, was dashed to pieces. Further south, the consequences were dire. The *Squirrel*, on her way from Newcastle to London with coals, was lost off Norfolk. Her master and 11 men were drowned. Three were saved. The *Good Intent*, on passage from Hartley to London with coals, also came to grief in the waters off Norfolk. She too lost her captain and this time six men were drowned. Three men lived to recount the events of that perilous episode.

The year 1803 also witnessed other spells of treacherous weather for seamen along the East Coast. In late September, for instance, a strong east-by-north gale, combined with rain, put the *Fame*, of London, which was in ballast, in trouble. She was driven on to the rocky shore near St Mary's Island, Whitley Bay, but the crew were saved.

At about the same time another vessel, the *Providence*, of Newcastle, was being blown towards Whitburn Rocks. Her master, Captain Carter, ordered two anchors dropped. But the anchors would not hold and he was forced to cut the cables. By good fortune, combined no doubt with skilled seamanship, the *Providence* managed to reach the safety of Sunderland harbour.

On the 11th of the month another strong gale hit vessels along the East Coast. The *Melton*, of Newcastle, under the command of a Captain Cram, lost all her boats and had three planks of her main deck torn up by the heavy seas. The ship's carpenter was washed overboard and drowned.

During a heavy gale in October 1803 the ship *Mary and Margaret*, of South Shields, was wrecked near Lowestoft. The crew were rescued. The next month brought another drama. The collier *Bee*, of North Shields, under the command of Captain John Houston, left her home port with a cargo of coals but was driven back by a strong south-easterly gale. As she attempted to re-enter the Tyne she tried to ride over the Bar but struck the sand among the breakers. The *Bee* was then swept on to the rocks at the Spanish Battery. The vessel was now in danger of being smashed to pieces by the huge waves which pounded her. The *Northumberland* lifeboat was launched,

manned by a crew of South Shields pilots, who managed to manoeuvre their craft with great skill among the rocks and awesome waves. The crew of six, including the master who was injured, were all rescued. 'Of all the daring attempts made with this boat, this was certainly the most hazardous,' commented the *Newcastle Courant*. 'Hundreds of spectators witnessed the scene and were greatly surprised by the boat scarcely shipping any water.'

Early January 1806 saw two ships driven on to the rocks of the Spanish Battery, the colliers *John and Richard* and *Leander*, both of Newcastle, which had been attempting to enter harbour. The *John and Richard* was broken to pieces soon after she struck.

The following month it was reported that the *Argo*, of Sunderland, which had been carrying coals, had been driven aground near Great Yarmouth in sight of a crowd of people on the beach. The vessel struck sands close to Gorleston and was smashed to pieces amongst the waves. Six of the crew, three of whom were seen clinging to the main mast, were washed overboard and disappeared. The remaining seven managed to reach the shore, where the master and one crewman died. The mate and four young men were the only survivors.

Late January 1815 witnessed another fierce storm, on this occasion accompanied by snow. The brig *Success* was struck by a tremendous sea as she came into the Tyne, her masts were broken away and she was driven on to the Herd Sand. The crew, except the helmsman, were swept into the water. Six men were saved by *The Original* lifeboat. The master, mate and a boy were drowned.

This storm raged on into the following day and the brig *Mercury*, of Blyth, struck the Black Middens rocks as heavy waves and surf continued to pound the coast. Again, *The Original* lifeboat went into action and saved the entire crew. The lifeboat suffered damage as she was dashed against the rocks.

Further north, the month of January had seen the *City of*

Aberdeen, a brig on passage from Sunderland to Aberdeen with coal, driven ashore on Holy Island. The crew were saved by island fishermen. The *Lark,* of Kings Lynn, also carrying a cargo of coal, was blown ashore and wrecked between Howick Burn and Boulmer. Five men and a boy were drowned.

The *Fountain,* of Sunderland, ran aground near her home port. All the crew were washed overboard to their deaths, except the ship's boy, who was found drowned in a cabin.

The *Durham Packet,* of Sunderland, carrying coal, came ashore near Clay in Norfolk. A faithful dog was sent by the crew to carry a line to the beach. But the shore was steeply shelving and the backwash of the breakers began to defeat his efforts. Two men on the beach saw the poor animal struggling from exhaustion. They went into the rough sea, risking their lives, and rescued the dog, who still loyally held the line in his mouth. The line link with the shore led to the rescue of all nine people aboard the *Durham Packet,* including two children. The brave dog had done a good day's work.

In April 1815 the colliers *Eleanor,* of Wallsend, and the *Noble,* of South Shields, were reported lost in a heavy gale while laden with coals. The crews were missing, feared dead. Two North Shields ships and their crews were also missing. Boats from these vessels were washed ashore in Norfolk.

The following month came another casualty. The brig *Providence,* on passage between Newcastle and Yarmouth, was wrecked at Winterton in Norfolk. The captain, his daughter, four seamen and a boy were rescued. One man was swept from the deck and drowned before a rope could be thrown aboard.

The *Louisa,* of London, bound from the Tyne to her home port with coal in January 1817, was damaged during a strong gale off Flamborough Head. Her master, a Captain Wilson, decided to return to the Tyne, but as she attempted to enter the river mouth the ship struck the Tyne Bar. She managed to free herself and got into deeper water. The *Louisa* sank barely five minutes after the crew took to the boat. They were safely picked up by another collier.

March 1820 witnessed the loss of the *Friendship,* of Sunderland, and the *Economy,* of Newcastle, wrecked on sands in southern waters during a spell of stormy weather. Most of the crews survived. The men of the *Economy* took to the boat as their ship began to break up. They tried rowing towards the land but became exhausted and cold. Luckily, they were spotted by boatmen from Ramsgate and landed at that port. Of the 11 crew, four had died from exposure.

In June of that year the *Mary Ann,* of Newcastle, came to grief on Haisborough Sand, off the Norfolk coast. All aboard lost their lives, except for the ship's carpenter, Robert Blueman, of South Shields, who was saved by the *Iroquois,* of Whitby, commanded by an appropriately named Captain Storm. The seaman had clung to a piece of the wreckage along with two shipmates, but they were washed off and disappeared. Captain Storm eventually transferred Robert Blueman to a Shields vessel, the master of which turned out to be Robert's father.

On the morning of May 11 1822 the collier *Enterprize,* of North Shields, was driven ashore at Ryhope, Sunderland, in a heavy east-south-east to east-north-east gale. Her master, a Captain Hadaway, and four crewmen were drowned. Four other crewmen and a passenger were saved. She was smashed to pieces as the tide rose.

The passenger, a Mr Dalton, gave this rare eyewitness account to the *Newcastle Courant*:

> The brig *Enterprize*, of North Shields, Edward Hadaway, master and owner, sailed for London, coal laden, on the morning of Thursday, the 9th inst., and after experiencing the dreadful gale on Friday, and reaching as far south as Whitby, was found at nine in the evening of that day to have drifted back abreast of Sunderland lighthouse, and on again standing to the southward, was on Saturday morning at one o'clock, the wind about east by south blowing a hurricane, with a tremendous sea, driven on shore between two ridges of rocks on Ryhope Sand.
>
> The crew, now nine in number (one having been washed overboard on Friday morning), and a passenger (Mr Dalton), took to the rigging and there remained, when about half past six the decks broke up, and the ship separating from the stern to the windlass, the mainmast went overboard, on which were the captain and the other three, all of whom perished.
>
> Shortly after the foremast carried away, on which were the mate and cook, the former succeeded in quitting the wreck of the mast and gained the forecastle – the latter being quite exhausted, failed and sank forever.
>
> The peasantry, at this time (about 7 o'clock) appearing on the beach, the remaining four and the passenger, then clinging to the bowsprit and forecastle, were by the assistance of cords thrown to them from the shore, drawn from their perilous situation and apparently inevitable death.
>
> The almost lifeless survivors were then conducted to Mr Robson's Salutation Inn, Ryhope, where they received the most human and christian-like treatment, as well as from Warren Maude Esq., and Capt. Dale, the former by the ample present of necessary clothing, the latter by his kind and sympathetic attention and refreshment, consequently, the whole must have the most heartfelt gratitude of each surviving individual.

A strong gale swept the waters of the North Sea in October 1824. The wind blew from the east and north-east. A number of colliers from North Shields were reported driven ashore near the mouth of the Tees. The captain of the *Aurora* and eight of his men were drowned off Easington. The *Paragon,* under the command of a Captain Smith, was reported to have broken to pieces after grounding. Nine colliers from Sunderland were ashore at Hartlepool.

The *Jenny* and the *William and Mary,* both of South Shields, were wrecked near Easington. Four men from the *Jenny* were drowned, but the rest of the crew saved. The men of the *William and Mary* were all rescued.

In October 1829 a number of loaded colliers sailed from Sunderland with a fine north-westerly wind to help them on their way south. But when night fell the wind veered to the north-east and the sea became rough. The morning brought the inevitable catalogue of wrecks. By 3pm, 15 ships were ashore between the South Pier at the mouth of the Wear and Hendon. The lifeboat was kept busy and saved all the crews. However, a sloop, which had sailed northwards and attempted to return to Sunderland, sank off the mouth of the harbour and all aboard were lost.

In January 1843 the snow *Percy* was on her way into South Shields from London when she came to grief on the Black Middens rocks. The *Percy* began to break up. Her master, a Captain Hair, the ship's boy and the cook tried to swim ashore but were drowned as they did so. The rest of the crew were saved by a seaman, William Wheeler, who managed to reach the wreck in a boat. At about the same the *Isabellas,* a Sunderland ship, struck the Spanish Battery rocks and was damaged beyond repair.

These were by no means all the colliers wrecked off the North-East coast in that year. A strong south-easterly gale in late September drove 17 Tyne ships ashore at Stranton Beach, Hartlepool. The crew of a vessel named the *Albion* were missing, presumed drowned.

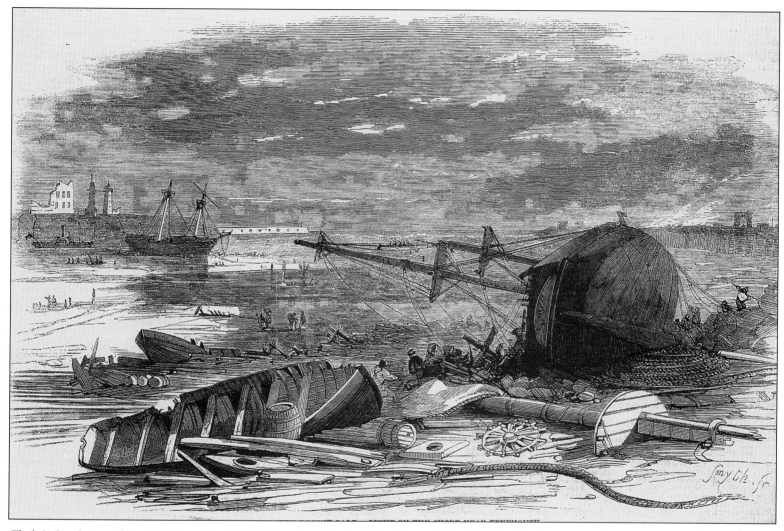

*The brig **Sarah Ann,** of South Shields, pictured right, lies on her side after being driven on to the Herd Sand during a strong gale in 1861. Her crew were saved by the lifeboats. The **Sarah Ann** was refloated, repaired and sold to Whitby owners in 1864. The following year she sank after a collision off Flamborough Head.*

One of the worst disasters at the mouth of the Tyne occurred in December 1849. The *Providence* lifeboat overturned in stormy conditions while trying to rescue the crew of the brig *Betsy* which had run aground on the Herd Sand. Twenty men, all pilots who had been manning the lifeboat, were drowned, leaving many widows and children.

In early April 1850 a large fleet of colliers bound for the Tyne came to grief in an unusual way. There were said to be between 400 and 500 of these ships. For weeks previously they had been held up in Yarmouth Roads by adverse winds. However, eventually the wind shifted to the south-east in the form of a welcoming breeze and the great fleet departed northwards. But the breeze gradually increased to a strong gale which whipped up heavy seas.

As they approached the mouth of the Tyne conditions were appalling. At first, three ships were driven on to the rocks near the Spanish Battery but the crews survived. However, as the great mass of vessels came running into the harbour before the wind many were out of control and numerous collisions occurred with heavy damage. The Narrows were clogged with ships wrecked as a result of crashing into one another. Steam tugs were brought in to clear them and the task took several days.

February 1861 was a day to remember for many people at South Shields. A heavy gale blew the schooner *Fowlis*, entering harbour after a voyage from Inverness, on to the Herd Sand. She then drifted on to the stones by the South Pier. Four lifeboats attempted to reach the vessel but were unable to get alongside her. The lifeboat *Providence* was badly damaged in one of these attempts. But the rescuers did not give up. The lifeboat *Tyne* managed to fire a rocket line to the *Fowlis* and the captain and mate were saved. Then the line broke. Four crewmen remained aboard the stricken vessel. One of these managed to swim to the lifeboat and was rescued.

A crowd of people ashore watched the remaining three clinging to the ship, unable to do anything to help. The lifeboats battled on for three hours in several attempts to rescue them. As the gale steadily increased the ship began to break up. Two of the men were swept to their deaths amongst the wreckage. The third was luckily washed towards the shore and a line was thrown to him. He caught it and was pulled to safety. The crowd cheered.

The *Fowlis* was one of several vessels wrecked that day at the mouth of the Tyne. For instance, the brig *Sarah Ann*, of South Shields, came ashore on the Herd Sand but her crew were rescued by the hard-worked lifeboats. Two days later the ship was refloated and later repaired. Altogether, it was estimated that around 50 ships had been driven on to the coast between South Shields and Whitby.

Ironically, the Herd Sand, which had proved to be the graveyard of so many ships, was, for a short time at least, navigable. In August 1820 it was reported that since January of that year the depth of water over the sand had been increasing and that there was a passage across it into the harbour. 'It is curious to see ships navigating in safety across the Herd Sand,' declared the *Newcastle Courant*. This was just one example of how over the years sands and channels could and still do shift.

In 1808 the towers of the new High and Low Lights at North Shields were completed. They began operating in 1810. These two lights, when aligned one above another, still help to lead vessels safely into the Tyne through deep water. Those beacons shining out from the land must have seemed to the collier sailors like loyal friends welcoming them home from the perils of the deep. Yet no light could ever protect a sailing ship from the furies of a storm or gale driving her relentlessly towards an uncertain fate on a shore of the East Coast.

~The Bold Privateer~

The Napoleonic Wars were an extremely dangerous time for the men of the North-East colliers. Marauding French privateers captured many ships and also took crews as prisoners of war. The privateers sold the captured vessels and their cargoes, with only some of the profits going to the French government. It was a lucrative but dangerous activity, akin to piracy.

Royal Navy warships fought back against the privateers and sometimes managed to re-take ships that had been captured. As time went on they became more successful in combating this menace to Britain's merchant fleet.

The *Newcastle Courant* spoke of the success of these enemy raiders: 'The French privateers are fast sailing luggers, and in the case of a calm or little wind they are provided with sweeps (oars), which renders it a matter of difficulty, if not impossible, to come up with them. Besides, the plans they proceed upon are of a nature so secure that it is a rare chance for our cruisers to get a sight of them.

'As soon as it is dusk, they put out from Dunkirk, or the adjacent ports, whether favoured by breeze or not; by midnight they are in the track of our vessels passing up and down the Channel and seldom fail to pick up a prize or two that pays well for their active speculation. They have themselves little to lose, for a privateer, and all on board, is seldom worth £200. The temptation, on the other hand is great, as they frequently capture vessels, which, with their cargoes, are estimated at £20,000.'

Those seamen who became prisoners of war would be transferred from their own vessel to the ship of the privateer and taken back to France or Holland. Frenchmen would then man the merchant vessel, with the help of perhaps one or two British crewmen left aboard, and take her into port as a prize.

Understandably, many colliers began carrying guns. Sometimes they fought back against these sea raiders and succeeded in beating them off. An example occurred as early as January 1798 when the *Vine*, of Sunderland, carrying coals from Sunderland to Portsmouth, was taken off Dungeness in the Channel by a privateer.

The raider, flying Danish colours, hailed them in good English. The master told the crew of the *Vine* that he would send them some gin on board. But when a boat arrived from the privateer it contained a French captain and 17 armed men.

Ten French crewmen were left aboard the *Vine* to steer the ship to Dunkirk. As dawn broke the next day the master of the *Vine*, Captain Graydon, decided to retake his ship. But only the mate, a James Liddell, obeyed the order to seize the pistols. Even so, for a short while they had possession of the vessel again.

However, it appears that there was a struggle with the French, the pistol barrels snapped and the mate's thumb was cut off. Captain Graydon was also wounded. The two men were forced to surrender and the French re-took the ship. The *Vine* arrived at Dunkirk the next day and the master was sent to prison. However, he was later taken to hospital and from there he escaped, eventually crossing the Channel and arriving at Romney.

Another fight-back against the enemy occurred in March 1799 when the *Shafto*, of Newcastle, on her way to London with

Shipping crowds the mouth of the Tyne at North Shields with the Low and High Lights visible. In the distance are the ruins of Tynemouth Castle and Priory. Drawing: J.W. Carmichael. Engraver: Lambert & Collard.

coal, was intercepted by a lugger privateer carrying 16 guns as she lay at anchor off East Anglia. The *Shafto*, however, had six guns of her own and as the crew saw the privateer bearing down on them, they prepared to fire. Soon, the French found themselves subjected to an unexpected broadside. The privateer turned and sailed away without returning a shot. The men of the *Shafto* cheered and fired off one of their guns in defiant celebration of their enemy's flight.

An account of a clash with a privateer is given in a letter, dated December 30 1800, written to the *Newcastle Courant* by a Captain Humble, master of the *Milburn*, of North Shields. He wrote: 'Yesterday we had a warm action with a French schooner privateer of 14 guns off Whitby. The enemy came boldly up within 30 yards of our broadside and fired into us; we returned his salute by firing our great guns and musketry for half an hour, as fast as we could load and discharge, when the privateer sheered off. I am satisfied we did him much damage before he left us, and am happy to say none of us are any worse, except myself, wounded in the hand by one of our own firearms.

'I cannot say too much in praise of my whole crew, they gallantly stood to their quarters during the whole time of the battle. The battle had scarce ceased an hour when another cutter privateer hove in sight, on which we thought it prudent to bear away for Scarbro.'

The mere appearance or the firing of warning shots by a British warship would have probably been enough to cause privateer seamen to quit a captured ship and take to their own vessels, rapidly melting into the horizon. Understandably, they did not feel it worth risking their lives or possible capture when there were so many other vessels to be taken on the sea, out of sight of the Royal Navy. Privateers liked easy pickings.

Yet, although the raiders might be extremely reluctant to fight a warship, they were not averse, as we have seen, to engaging a single merchant vessel in a battle. Groups of merchant ships were another matter. For instance, in 1804 the

William and Mary, of South Shields, under the command of a Captain Robinson, fought a musket and cannon battle with a privateer for three hours off the Tees. Capt Robinson had been promised assistance from two other British merchant ships but they sailed away without firing a gun. The *William and Mary* was forced to strike (surrender).

The *Courant* declared: 'Had they rendered only trivial aid the privateer would have sheered off, as they were informed by the crew of the enemy when boarded. One of the master's hands was shattered, but medical assistance was given by surgeons aboard the privateer, when the prisoners were shifted.

'The *William and Mary* had 11 Frenchmen put on board of her, and one man and a boy of her own crew left on board. She had sustained so much injury in the action that she went down, and only the Englishman and two Frenchmen were saved in the boat. The Englishman is since arrived in South Shields.'

In March 1804 the laden collier *Scipio*, of North Shields, was attacked by a sloop-rigged privateer off Cromer, Norfolk. The French poured in musket fire and then cannon, but the crew of *Scipio* fought back. The action was said to have lasted nearly an hour.

The collier then managed to escape to Yarmouth Roads where she arrived with her sails and rigging damaged. A musket ball had gone through one of the *Scipio* captain's feet. His wound was dressed by a surgeon from HMS *Irresistible* anchored at Great Yarmouth.

Several privateer crews managed to combine smuggling with their more 'official' activities. Sailing in cutters and luggers they ran spirits into places such as Boulmer, Holy Island, Robin Hood's Bay, and Runswick Bay. On their way back home they would turn privateer and take one or two undefended colliers. The distinction between privateers, smugglers and pirates was at times a fine line.

As usual in warfare, surprise attacks were a tactic sometimes employed. The *Providence*, of South Shields, was captured in a raid in October 1805 by a lugger privateer disguised as a fishing boat off the Suffolk coast. The crew were working aloft at the time, reefing the top-sails. The raiders on this occasion were carrying only small arms. The *Courant* warned: 'Ships at sea should always have their guns loaded, and clear for battle, and suspect everything that comes near them. It is often by stealth or strategem that light colliers are boarded.'

Many North-East collier seamen became prisoners in France as a result of the raids. In 1807, for instance, the town of South Shields sent a subscription to Lloyd's of London for the relief of these unfortunate men. It totalled £187, of which the Dean and Chapter of Durham gave £20. The following year it was reported that many of the insurance societies on the Tyne had decided to contribute towards the relief funds. On this occasion, more than £65 was donated.

Some prisoners of war, however, managed to escape. In June 1812 nine men were landed at Sandgate in Kent from a schooner. They had been rescued at sea after escaping from a prison at Verdun via a sewer. Forty-eight men had originally escaped but some had been shot and others recaptured by the French. One of those who reached Britain was said to be a Shields man, part owner of the ship *Neptune.* He had been wounded in the leg.

Of all the privateer captains who cruised the waters of the North Sea and Channel, 'Citizen Blackman', as he was known (his real name may have been Blancman) was said to be the most successful and he therefore also became the most notorious. He was reported to have a whole 'fleet' of ships under his command and was sometimes referred to as 'Commodore Blackman'. His base was Dunkirk and other ports nearby.

In November 1800 the mysterious commodore, in his 14-gun vessel the *Chasseur,* captured six ships bound from the Tyne to London. They were the *Free Briton,* of Newcastle, the *Dorset,* of Shields, the *Nile,* of Newcastle, the *Hope,* the *William*

and Betsy, and another vessel named the *Hope,* all from Sunderland. They had been taken off the Cromer Light, Norfolk. However, the *Rover,* a British lugger, bravely managed to re-take one of the ships and brought her safely into Great Yarmouth. The bold Captain Blackman escaped with the rest of the vessels and took them to Boulogne.

The *Newcastle Courant* declared: 'Citizen Blackman, alias Blanckman, has of late made many depredations on the East Coast of Britain, and is now as famous as the celebrated Capt. Delatre. He generally makes his cruises in the months of November, December, January and February, and commonly towards the change of moon.'

Writing to his brother from Holland in 1800, a Mr R. Fell, of London, who was captured by Blackman while sailing in the Whitby sloop *Active,* told of the privateers: 'Never did a more rascally gang of cut-throats put to sea than the crew of the *Chasseur.* The utmost vigilance and circumspection has been necessary on my part to prevent my being murdered, but for a dreadful gale of wind which furnished them with other employment, I should be this time have been in heaven; and what had been the lot of my wife and other females in the vessel I shudder to think of.'

In January 1801 came another report of a sea raid by Citizen Blackman. This time the *Edgar,* on passage to the Tyne from London, and the *Eagle,* bound for the Tyne from the Baltic, both North Shields-owned ships, were captured off Spurn Head. Shortly afterwards, Blackman, commanding what may have been a small squadron of ships, took the *Robert,* of Blyth, which was carrying coal, and the *Robert and Margaret,* of Newcastle.

Later in the month, Blackman's privateers were still raiding the East Coast. On this occasion he captured several laden vessels off Spurn Head and took them to France and Holland. However, there were signs that the Royal Navy was now fighting back against him. The sloop-of-war *Ranger* sailed to the Dutch coastal waters and re-took one of the ships, the *Friends,* of North Shields. On sighting the *Ranger* bearing down on them the Frenchmen left the ship by boarding a boat and escaped to the shore. Only two boys were found on board the *Friends*. There is little doubt that the rest of the crew had been made prisoners of war.

The brig *Isis,* of Shields, was also reported captured at about the same time. She was re-taken by the British armed brig *Sally*. The privateers fled in their ship and the *Sally* gave chase but could not catch up with her.

Not long after these incidents, Blackman's ship, the *Chasseur,* was pursued in the Channel by the frigate *Shannon*. The privateer captain was evidently determined that both he and his vessel would not be caught. He ran his ship ashore on to the sands near Calais. It was the end of the *Chasseur,* but not of Captain Blackman. A report stated that after this episode he became ill with fever and had not sailed out of France for some time.

But the sea-going 'Citizen' recovered from this malady. By March 1801 he had found a ship to replace the wrecked *Chasseur*. This time he commanded a vessel named the *Bellona,* said to carry 19 or 20 guns.

His first reported prize sailing in the *Bellona* was the *Lady Stormont*, bound from Dundee to London, with a valuable cargo. On this cruise he also took six colliers on passage from the North-East to London. They were the *Thames*, which had sailed from Newcastle, and the *Hope's Increase*, the *Jean*, the *Lively,* the *Susannah* and the *Providence,* all from Sunderland. At about the same time Blackman also captured the laden collier *Thomas and Betsy*, of Sunderland. But she was re-taken by two fishing smacks and brought safely into Harwich.

In November 1804 the collier *Bridget* arrived in Shields harbour with more news of the intrepid 'Citizen'. The master of the *Bridget,* a Captain Gardner, reported that he had been hailed by the ship *Contents Increase*, of North Shields, and told that the vessel had been captured a couple of days previously by Captain Blackman near Spurn Head. The British gun brig *Minx* had re-taken the *Contents Increase*. Blackman was said to

have a squadron of ships with him.

In early November 1804 the by now almost legendary French commander was reported to have captured the Newcastle ship *Belisarius* off Tynemouth Castle. The crew were sent to Dunkirk as prisoners.

Towards the end of that year, possibly late November or early December, the British brig-cutter *Cruizer* sighted Citizen Blackman's ship (by now he was apparently sailing in a vessel named the *Contre-Admiral Magon*) and chased her for 100 miles. The chase ended with her being driven ashore near Great Yarmouth. The privateer commander was at last captured.

What became of Citizen Blackman does not seem to be recorded, so it is not known whether he died a prisoner in England or eventually managed to return to his native land.

However, there was possibly a more humane side to the character of the 'rascally' French commander than contemporary accounts of him would suggest. In April 1801, the laden collier *Brotherly Love*, commanded by Captain Joseph Graham, of South Shields, was captured by a privateer. The collier had nine South Shields pilots aboard who were going southward in search of ships returning to port in ballast.

The *Newcastle Courant* told of the encounter: 'The French captain was very kind to them; he regaled them with claret, gave them their cobles again and yesterday morning they arrived at Shields.' Perhaps this 'kind' captain was the mysterious Citizen Blackman, scourge of the British merchant fleet.

Figureheads

Figureheads were carried on the stem of the ship below the bowsprit by many colliers and were often painted white. Old sailors looked upon these models as the eyes of the ship, without which she could not find her way. A ship is traditionally referred to as a 'she' and in the 19th century female figureheads were the most popular. It was also believed that a naked woman could tame a storm and bared breasts feature in many of these symbolic adornments.

The figurehead below is from the collier *Light of the Harem* which was wrecked on the shore at Tynemouth during a gale in February 1870. People carried off coal and other items washed ashore from the vessel and from two other ships also wrecked at the river mouth.

The figurehead above is from the snow *First of May*. She was bound from London to the Tyne in ballast in December 1876 when she was struck by a huge sea as she was entering the river during a severe easterly gale. Her steering and rigging were disabled and she drifted helplessly into Prior's Haven, Tynemouth. The crew were saved by members of the Tynemouth Volunteer Life Brigade who fired a line to the ship.

The *First of May* was uninsured. The ship had been built at Monkwearmouth, Sunderland, in 1855. She was one of seven vessels wrecked at the mouth of the Tyne during a spell of bad weather. Thirty seamen were reported drowned.

The figureheads shown here can be seen in the Volunteer Life Brigade Watch House at Tynemouth.

The Schooner *Sally*

*The **Sally** sailed regularly to London and to France in the coal trade.*

*The extracts below are from the logbook of the **Sally** commanded by Thomas Wallace.*

*The **Sally** was on passage from the Tyne to London in June 1845, with about 212 tons of coal.*

*The **Sally** was advertised for sale in the **Newcastle Courant** on 18 May 1840.*

June 10th. At 6pm towed from the Spouts to sea by the *Collingwood* steamer. At 8.30 discharged the steamer; made all sail; light winds West. At 5am in studding sails; light wind SSE.

June 11th. The whole of these 24 hours fine pleasant weather with light winds at S by E, ship flying to windward.

June 12th. The whole of these 24 hours fine and pleasant weather with light winds and variable. Midnight Flamborough Head, bearing south.

June 13th. These 24 hours light airs with calms at intervals. Midnight Flambro Head Light, bearing NW.

June 14th. Commenced light airs ENE set the studding sails. At 6pm thick foggy weather; more clear at 8pm. Foggy weather.

June 15th. Commenced foggy and calm. At 2am more clear; set fore topmast studding sail. Light air E by N. At 8am in studding sail. Wind SE. Dudgeon Light bearing SE by S. Tacked ship to the eastwards. At 4pm tacked ship to the SSW. Midnight light winds SSE.

June 16th. Commenced light winds SSE, ship plying to windward. At 4pm came to anchor in 10 fathoms water. Low water. Got under weigh; flying to windward.

June 17th Commenced light wind South. Ship flying to windward. Came to anchor off Cromer in 8 fathoms. Low water underweigh.

June 18th. Commenced light wind variable. At 8pm came to anchor in the Cockle Gatt [off Winterton]. Midnight light wind ESE.

June 19th. Commenced light wind SE. At 3am got underweigh, proceeded through roads [Yarmouth Roads]. At 7am came to anchor in Lowestoft Roads. Thick foggy weather. Low water got underweigh. Winds variable. At 11pm came to anchor in 7 fathoms. Wind NW light winds.

June 20th. At 3am got underweigh. Winds variable from WNW to SSE. Midnight came to anchor in sea reach. Low water got underweigh. Wind ESE proceeded up river [Thames].

~Danger on the Waves~

To be driven onto the rocks or sand of a lee shore or captured by a privateer were not the only dangers faced by the collier crews. For example, collisions between ships at sea or in rivers might have fatal consequences, a vessel might spring a leak or hazards of the weather might set a ship adrift in the open sea.

On May 12 1808 the brig *Hope*, of South Shields, commanded by a Captain John Hodge, was run down while carrying coal at 1am, about 15 miles to the south of Flamborough Head, Yorkshire. The captain and seven of his crew lost their lives. The ship which hit them did not stop nor did her crew send a boat to assist the stricken *Hope*. The mystery vessel simply sailed away. A 50 guineas reward was offered for information leading to the identification of the ship.

Another tragic collision occurred in November 1807 when the collier *Bell*, of Newcastle, was on her way to London. She was in collision with the *Newcastle Packet*, which traded between Newcastle and the capital. Both vessels had apparently been steering to avoid another ship which was between them. The *Bell* was badly damaged and she sank less than five minutes after the impact.

The crew managed to swim towards the *Packet* and were safely picked up. Sadly, a man, his wife and three children, who had been passengers in the *Bell*, did not manage to evacuate the ship in time and were drowned.

The ordeal of being adrift in an open boat was suffered by men from the collier *Pearl*, which departed from the Tyne with coals for Copenhagen in May 1803. When out to sea, the ship began to leak and this was evidently no mere trickle. The crew

of 14 manned the pumps but the sea poured in as fast as they could pump it out.

The *Pearl* was now in danger of sinking and the men launched the boat over the side in preparation for abandoning ship. However, the boat was damaged as it fell and they found themselves taking to the sea in a craft with a hole in its side. The *Pearl* sank 10 minutes after the men quit the vessel.

They were now in an extremely dangerous position. They had no sail, only one oar, and no food or drink. They tried to stop up the hole with their jackets, but it was to no avail. Day and night the crew were forced to bail the craft out using their hats.

On the third day of being adrift 10 of the men died of hunger, thirst and fatigue. According to the *Newcastle Courant*, the four survivors were forced to 'subsist on parts of their dead comrades'. On the fifth day the boat drifted ashore at Thorpe on the Norfolk coast. One man died soon after landing but the three others lived to recount the tale of their harrowing experience.

Tragedy could also strike in a literal sense. On April 13 1821 a thunder storm broke as the collier *Captain Cook*, of North Shields, commanded by a Captain Armstrong, was off Scarborough. Two young and evidently greatly valued apprentices were struck dead by lightning while they were taking in the fore-top-gallant sail. Both boys were aged about 16. One fell to the deck and the other into the sea. It was reported that the smell of sulphur lingered for some time about the ship after this sad accident.

But sometimes there were happy endings to ordeals on the

*Unusual mishap. Two brigs are seen jammed together at the entrance lock to the East India Docks, Blackwall, London, in June 1858. On the right, is the **Lustre,** of South Shields, a collier inbound with a cargo of 'black diamonds'. The other vessel is the **Ocean,** of Shoreham, which was attempting to leave the docks. Both ships leaned over towards one another and the **Lustre** caused damaged to the sides of the **Ocean** because of her weighty cargo. The starboard side of the **Ocean** had to be cut away to loosen the jam. The **Lustre** was eventually towed out of the lock by a tug. Both vessels were badly damaged.*

The High Light is depicted in this atmospheric, twilight view of North Shields.

waves. There has always been an unwritten code of the sea that sailors should help fellow mariners in distress. An example of such kindness can be found in the case of the *Betsy*, which sailed from Newcastle laden with coals for Montrose on February 28 1818. It proved to be a rough and hazardous passage. The *Betsy* was tossed about and before long she had lost her bowsprit, jib, and the boat. Many other moveable items of equipment on deck were washed overboard in the heavy seas.

By March 13, after being at sea for two weeks, the ship's food and drink had nearly run out. The men were, not surprisingly, close to the end of their endurance with fatigue and hunger. They then sighted a vessel running to the eastward which spotted their signal of distress and sailed towards them.

The ship was the *Peggy*, of Kincardine, commanded by an aptly named Captain Scotland. The captain sent over a boat with provisions for the men of the *Betsy*. This kind and generous action of providing food and drink saved their lives. The *Betsy* eventually arrived at Montrose on March 22, nearly a month after setting out. All the crew had survived. The humanitarian code of the sea had been followed in exemplary fashion.

The brig **Susannah Thrift,** built in Newcastle in 1865 was owned by Robert Thrift of Blyth and after 1888 by Matthew Pearson of South Shields. On the 13th October 1899 she foundered following a collision with the Belgian steamship **Leopold II** when on a voyage from the Tyne to Cowes, Isle of Wight, with coal.

~Heralds of Steam~

On June 30 1852 the steam-driven, iron-hulled screw collier *John Bowes* was launched into the Tyne from the shipyard of Palmer Bros & Co at Jarrow. The event signalled the beginning of the decline and fall of the sailing ship on the East Coast coal runs. The vessel is generally regarded as the most important pioneer of steam in the 'black diamonds' trade.

However, the *John Bowes* was not the first steam-driven vessel to carry coal. In 1841 the iron screw steamer *Bedlington*

*Charles Palmer, the shipbuilder whose ideas led to the launch of the pioneering steam collier **John Bowes** in 1852.*

was built for the Bedlington Coal Company and operated for a time on the River Blyth and between the port of Blyth and the Tyne. Later, in 1844, an iron screw steamer known as the *Q.E.D.* was launched at the yard of John Coutts in Walker, Newcastle. She is known to have carried coal.

The following year a wooden-hulled steamer, the *Experiment*, was completed at Sunderland and also made a number of coal voyages to the capital. But it was the *John Bowes* which created the greatest impact and became by far the most commercially successful of these pioneering vessels.

The advent of the ship with a steam engine linked to a screw propeller meant that coal could be delivered to its destination with a regularity and speed which a sailing collier could not match, dependent as she was on the vagaries of the weather. A steamship did not need to wait for a favourable wind.

Ironically, the launch of the *John Bowes* had been prompted by competition from steam on the land. The development of railways led to the fast delivery of coal to London and the South-East from pits in the northern Midlands and Yorkshire. Steam trains delivered 8,000 tons of coal to the capital in 1845. The amounts then began to increase dramatically. The year 1848 saw 38,000 tons delivered by train. In 1851 the figure reached 248,000 tons.

Mine owners in the North-East were worried by this challenge. There was even talk of delivering coal by rail from the Tyne to London. But Charles Palmer, a businessman born at South Shields and who had shares in North-East collieries, had other ideas. He believed that the land-based threat from steam

The launch of the iron screw steam collier **John Bowes** *at the Jarrow yard of Palmer Bros. & Co. on June 30 1852. This ship was the most important pioneer of steam on the East Coast coal runs. Equipped with two engines, she also carried sails. The* **John Bowes** *completed her first round voyage from the Tyne to London and back in seven days, even though her engines were running at little more than half speed. Her career was to last 81 years.*

could be met by using steam on the sea. Charles became one of the directors of a newly formed business, the General Iron Screw Collier Company, which he and others formed to operate steamers on the coal runs.

It was his belief in steam power which led to the launching of the *John Bowes* from the Jarrow shipyard in 1852. Charles had founded the shipyard with his brother, George, a year earlier. The *John Bowes* was only their second vessel but it helped to ensure the success of the new business. Within a few years

steam colliers were one of the mainstays of the yard.

The launch of the *John Bowes* was evidently a rather grand occasion. Coalowners and manufacturers were among the large number of people who attended the event. Guests included the Mayor and Sheriff of Newcastle. At 2.15 in the afternoon, which was high water, the 148ft-long ship glided into the Tyne without any major problem. The naming ceremony was performed by Charles's wife and afterwards the 200 official guests were given dinner at the yard. In the evening, Charles

*The **John Bowes** seen in the Tyne during her later years, c. late 1800s. Note, much of her original rigging has been removed. Her 81-year career ended in 1933 when she sank off the coast of northern Spain. The crew were saved.*

and the Mayor's wife led off the dancing.

The ship upon which the Palmer brothers had pinned their hopes proved to be a great success. She ushered in an era which saw steam colliers become a rapidly growing feature of the North-East coast and its rivers.

The *John Bowes* left the Tyne for the first time with a cargo of 500 tons of coal on July 27 1852 under the command of a Captain John Scott. She halted at Sunderland for compass adjustment. From there, it took her two days to reach London, two days to discharge her cargo in the Thames, and she was back in the Tyne on August 3. The round voyage had taken her only seven days, as against a sailing collier's usual month.

This had been achieved even though she had been 'running in' her new engines by operating them at little more than half speed. The halt at Sunderland and a slight collision with a French fishing smack off Whitby on the return run also added to her passage time. However, she was not carrying a full cargo. The 500 tons loaded was 150 tons short of her full hold capacity.

But the *John Bowes* had proved that the expense of building an iron steam collier, as opposed to a relatively inexpensive wooden sailing ship, was a sound economic proposition.

As if to hedge bets, the single-funnel vessel carried sails as well as engines. When the weather was favourable early steamships sometimes used the power of the wind to conserve fuel. Sails were also a good insurance in case of engine failure or the loss of a propeller. The new ship was therefore rigged as a topsail schooner with three masts, but it is not recorded to what extent she used wind power. A story is told that on one occasion she lost her propeller in southerly waters and managed to return to the Tyne in reasonably good time by sail.

Despite such a story, it was her machinery which was the reason for her fame on Tyneside and elsewhere. Two single-cylinder engines linked to the propeller shaft were initially installed, giving a total of 70 horsepower. This produced a speed of around eight or nine knots. They were built by the renowned firm of Robert Stephenson at Forth Banks, Newcastle. Later in her career these engines were replaced with improved machinery.

The next steam collier to be built by the Palmer yard was the *William Hutt,* launched on December 7 1852. By this time the business had secured orders for ten more coal-carrying steamships. The third such vessel launched was the *Northumberland,* completed the following year.

The Palmer brothers had found a winning combination – steam as the prime motive force, an iron hull and a large (60ft long) hatch to make loading and discharging of the 'black diamonds' easier and involving less need for trimming the cargo. Another asset was the installation of water ballast tanks in many of the steamships which cut down on the time-consuming loading and discharging of solid ballast which had contributed to the silting of the Tyne.

Building a successful iron steam collier was one thing, battling against the entrenched interests, practices and legislation of a coal carrying trade, moulded around the small wooden sailing ship, was another. One obstacle soon encountered was the Coal Turn Act. With scores of sailing colliers often awaiting their turn to load a cargo at the staiths of the Tyne, this Act had been introduced to prevent preference being given to any particular ship in the 'queues'.

Early in 1853 the *John Bowes* loaded a cargo of coal from spouts at a Tyne staith and sailed immediately for Grimsby. Her place under the spouts was taken by the South Shields-owned snow *William*. The *William* had only taken part of her cargo on board when the *John Bowes* returned. The snow was promptly hauled off the berth to allow the steamer under the spouts for a second time.

Understandably, the *William's* owners were unhappy with this treatment and, under the terms of the Turn Act, brought an action against the coal fitter they held to be responsible. He was fined £15 by the Coal Turn Commissioners.

The case had important implications for the steam collier owners. There was little point in having an expensive ship, capable of making rapid round voyages, which on returning to the Tyne was left to lie idle, awaiting her turn behind the antiquated sailing colliers. However, by the end of 1853 action had been taken by the steamship owners to combat the problem. A new staith, reserved solely for the steam colliers, was constructed on the river.

It was not long before the owners of these ships were powerful enough to take on the the vested interests. In 1865 the Coal Turn Act was repealed. At the other end of the run, on the Thames, similar 'turn' rules went out of use at about the same time.

Improvements were also made in the methods of unloading ships. In 1862 William Cory & Sons positioned a large pontoon in Woolwich Reach on the Thames for the steamers to discharge their coal. The pontoon was equipped with hydraulic cranes built by the Newcastle company of Tyneside engineer and industrialist William Armstrong. Each crane was capable of discharging 60 tons of coal per hour. Previously, by an old trade custom of the port, the shipper or purchaser had the power to restrict the unloading rate to 49 tons per day. The cranes came hand in hand with another improvement – the pontoon in Woolwich reach was equipped with gas lighting so that vessels could discharge at night.

Meanwhile, faster ships had been launched on the Tyne. In January 1856 the steam collier *General Codrington*, built by Charles Mitchell at Low Walker, Newcastle, delivered 600 tons of coal to London and returned to the Tyne in a record time of four days, seven hours.

But this record was to be broken. The year 1859 saw the Palmer yard build the *James Dixon,* a steamer which turned in an even better performance. She could carry 1,200 tons of coal and make the round voyage in three days, four hours.

*Early steam colliers were sometimes used for tasks other than carrying coal. The **William Hutt** is seen here in heavy seas working to lay a telegraph cable between Britain and Belgium in 1853. She was the second steam collier from the Palmer yard at Jarrow. In 1857 the **William Hutt** was in collision with the Dutch steamer **Sophie** off Dungeness in the Channel. Twelve passengers and crew of the **Sophie** lost their lives. The Tyne ship was damaged but picked up the survivors. The **William Hutt**'s career was cut short in 1864 when she sank during a fierce gale off the East Anglian coast. She had been on a voyage from Sunderland to London with coal. One crewman was picked up by a fishing smack, but the remaining 17 hands were all lost.*

The *James Dixon* made 57 voyages to London in one year, delivering a total of 62,842 tons of coal with a crew of 22 men. To accomplish this work with sailing colliers would have required 16 ships and 144 men.

In 1852, the year in which the *John Bowes* made her debut, 9,483 tons of coal was delivered from the Tyne to London by steam collier. By 1862 this amount had increased almost one hundred fold to 929,825 tons – all taken southwards by the growing fleet of steamships.

Small wonder that the era of the wooden sailing collier was fast drawing to a close by the 1870s, although such vessels were to linger on in rapidly diminishing numbers until the early years of the 20th century. They were still useful for delivering coal to small ports which could not handle the large steamers or in situations where fast delivery was not required.

But in the year 1877, probably for the first time since North-East vessels began carrying coal centuries before, no new-built sailing ships of any type were acquired by Tyne owners. The steam collier was the undisputed successor to sail.

The 1850s had seen the opening of enclosed docks with staiths capable of taking the steam colliers as well as sailing vessels. Northumberland Dock at Howdon was opened in 1857 and Tyne Dock at South Shields in 1859. Suitable staiths also came into operation at Whitehill Point, close to Northumberland Dock, in 1874.

Another scheme gave added impetus to the export of coal from the Tyne. This was the removal of Newcastle's low stone bridge and its replacement with the Swing Bridge, completed in 1876, which meant steam colliers could now journey further up river. This eventually led to the opening of the large Dunston Staiths in 1893.

The pioneering *John Bowes* steamed onwards through all these developments. Her career was to last 81 years and during her long lifetime she carried general cargoes as well as coal. At the outbreak of the Crimean War in 1854 she and other steam colliers were chartered at Shields to carry coal supplies to the Baltic Fleet.

The revolutionary vessel changed ownership several times and in the last years of her life her rigging was reduced. Finally, in 1933, while carrying a cargo of iron ore and now bearing the name *Villa Selgas,* she sank off the coast of northern Spain after developing a leak in rough seas. All the crew were saved.

By a strange irony, 1933 was also the year in which the Palmer shipbuilding business at Jarrow collapsed, sparking mass unemployment in the town. By that time, the era of the little wooden sailing colliers with their brave crews had long vanished beyond the horizons of the sea.

The early steam collier Q.E.D.

The Tyne and Fawdon Staith from Wallsend, looking up river. Artist: Edward Swinburne, engraved by F.C. Lewis.

~Sailing collier facts and figures~

During the two weeks beginning 1 June 1831, 41 Tyne-owned sailing colliers arrived in the Thames. They carried a total of 12,261 tons of coal. This was a typical number of arrivals for the time.

Average cargo carried: 299 tons of coal per vessel

Largest cargo: 445 tons

Average registered tonnage of ship: 217 tons

Average length: 84.1 feet

Average breadth: 24.3 feet

Average age: about 22 years

Snow rigged: 32

Brig rigged: 9

Built on the Tyne: 15

Built on the Wear: 8

Built at Stockton: 2

The distance by sea between Shields Harbour and the Tower of London is about 307 nautical miles or 354 statute miles.

The fastest recorded passage time by sailing ship (not a collier) between Shields Harbour and the Tower of London was 32 hours

Shipwrecks: Between 1830 and the end of the sailing ship era a staggering 70 per cent of all Tyne-owned sailing ships were lost through marine peril – wrecked by striking the shore, rock or shoal, sunk at sea, hit by fire or explosion, crushed by ice, sunk by collision or disappeared.

Loss of life: At the end of the 19th century it was estimated that one in five merchant seamen in the coastal trade lost their lives at sea.

Bibliography and a brief selection of further reading

Published sources

Finch, R. *Coals from Newcastle*, Lavenham, Suffolk, 1973
Keys, R.E. *The Sailing Ships of Aln & Coquet*, Newcastle, 1993
Keys, R.E. *A Dictionary of Tyne Sailing Ships*, publication pending
MacRae, J.A. and C.V. Waine, *The Steam Collier Fleets*, Waine Research Publications, reprint 1995
Osler, A. and A. Barrow, *Tall Ships Two Rivers*, Keepdate, Newcastle, 1993
Runciman, W. *Before the Mast – and After*, London, 1924
Runciman, W. *Collier Brigs and their Sailors*, London, 1926

Newspapers

Newcastle Chronicle
Newcastle Courant
Newcastle Journal
The Times

Periodicals

Illustrated London News
Maritime History
Sea Breezes

A brig and brigantine lie at their moorings. The brigantine, left, is drying her sails. The brig appears to be a very old vessel with a characteristic collier rig.